THE LITTLE BOOK OF ML

The Little Book of ML

(C) 2019 – Steve Piers

This book is protected by copyright. That said, I am more than happy for you to share it and I hope as many people as possible will see it and learn about Multi Level Marketing.

Please pass this book on to anyone you think will benefit from reading it. You can gift free copies to friends via Amazon Kindle Unlimited, or buy paper copies for the cheapest price the system will let me pick. Or scan it, photocopy it, I am more than happy for you to pass this on to anyone and let's make the world a better place.

A Point of View.

Before we begin, let's make it clear – everything you're about to read is an opinion based on experience, investigation and research. You may agree with the points I raise, or you may not. If you have started a Multi Level Marketing company and made billions of pounds then I dare say you will disagree with all of this.

But this book isn't aimed at them. This is for you – the potential new recruit that's been offered the opportunity to make money by joining a Multi Level Marketing scheme. The big question is, will **you** be the next person to make a fortune by joining one of these schemes?

I hope the information in this booklet will help you reach your own opinion before you consider joining any Multi Level Marketing scheme. It is a viewpoint that I believe will be helpful to you and I hope the content of the following pages helps you make an informed decision.

The Chain Letter.

When I was a kid, my Dad had a short conversation with me that I have never forgotten. At the time, some point in the 1980s, there had been resurgence in the popularity of Chain Letters and the narrative had taken a dark turn. People were receiving mail from strangers telling them to send money to people they didn't know, with the threat of bad luck forever if they failed to comply. It was discussed on the TV news and experts were brought in to explain why Chain Letters were a scam, why you shouldn't send any money to anyone and (most importantly for some superstitious people) that you would not receive bad luck for breaking the chain.

My Dad was explaining to me how the Chain Letter worked and confided that he had been involved in one himself in the 1950s. Back then the whole process was more innocent and the Chain Letter would explain the money making opportunities to the reader without the need to threaten those who may break the chain. I found the whole conversation fascinating and it seems intriguing to me now that as the Chain Letter movement is all but extinct today, pyramid schemes and Multi Level Marketing companies are springing up all over the place. There are so many similarities between all these schemes and it feels the right time to take a look at how these things work in more detail.

Step one in the creation of an original 1950s style, non-threatening Chain Letter was to create a list of names and addresses. You could get these from the telephone directory at random or include friends of friends, someone you saw in the local newspaper, anyone at all. Then you'd get out the trusty typewriter and write ten letters. The letter should be intriguing, piquing the interest of the reader. The letter would contain your list of nine random names and addresses with your own details somewhere in the middle. It goes something like this.

THE LITTLE BOOK OF MULTI LEVEL MARKETING

Dear (recipient's name)

I hope this letter finds you well. You don't know me, but I'm taking part in an experiment and I am pleased to say that I have selected you to join me in a quite frankly, unbelievable opportunity. As I write this I am receiving money through the post every day. I have more money than I ever believed possible and I am now sharing my wealth and good fortune with friends and family. I have given away so much money to those I love and I've decided to continue the scheme helping people I don't know. I saw in the local paper about the charity work you do and I feel that your tireless efforts should be rewarded. (*If you know something about the recipient this is a personal bit of information that makes the letter seem more specific to the individual*)

Below, there is a list of names and addresses of the other people I am helping. You will see name number one at the top of the list. This is the person that **you** will help and it is really easy to get involved. You should send £5 to the person at position number one on the list. Then, you should write ten letters, similar to this one, to anyone you wish to benefit from the scheme. In your letters, you should use the same list of names and addresses, but you must remove person number one, moving everyone up one position, then add your name at position ten. Here is your list:

1 – Alan Smithee – 22 Acacia Avenue, Bodshire

2 – (Bob – just a name and address from the phone book)

3 – (Claire , again it doesn't matter who)

4 – (Dawn - and so on)

5 – (Your name and address – because you're the person who started this Chain Letter)

6 – (another random name)

7 – (and so on)

8 – (and so on)

9 – (and so on)

10 – (and so on).

THE LITTLE BOOK OF MULTI LEVEL MARKETING

I am very excited that you are with us and in exchange for sending £5 to Alan Smithee and writing ten letters, you will receive riches beyond your wildest dreams – it is a mathematical certainty! I am serious about this, you can work it out with a calculator to check – we are talking millions of pounds.

Yours

The Wealth Creation Team

So, How does a Chain Letter work?

If everyone who receives the Chain Letter does as instructed, then the scheme will work – for a short while at least. However, whilst it is mathematically certain that the vast riches are going to flood in, the math is completely unsustainable for the overwhelming majority of the people who choose to take part. This includes everyone in the lower half of my original list and anyone who adds their name to it. Of course, as the founder of the Chain Letter it doesn't really matter to me if anyone makes any money or not as long as I make **my** money. Let's take a moment to understand the overall picture of what's really going to happen once I send my original ten letters.

First, we are going to assume that everyone who receives my letter responds. This is unlikely but I want to show the scheme in a best case scenario. I post my ten letters and the ten recipients decide this is a good plan and they want to be part of it. They each write ten letters, removing person number one from the list and adding their own name in position number ten. My name was at position number five, so in this new batch of letters, my name has moved up a level. That's 100 new letters going out in the mail, along with ten envelopes for Alan, each containing a five pound note. Alan has no idea why he has received it, but he's happy to receive random cash in the mail.

The chain continues and whilst Alan takes the family to Frankie and Benny's for a pizza, one hundred new people receive the new letter. Each of those new recipients follows the instructions. Between them, they mail 1000 letters, with my name at position three in the list. And Bob, the lucky person I randomly picked from the telephone directory for position 2 in my original list receives one hundred £5 notes. He takes the family to Benidorm.

The next level of the scheme involves the recipients of those 1000 letters placing my name at number two in the list and mailing 10 letters each. That's ten thousand letters in the mail, Claire receives £5000, pays for a new kitchen and my name is now at position number two.

This is starting to get out of hand, but at level 4, Dawn receives FIFTY THOUSAND POUNDS which isn't bad for a scheme that she didn't realise she was participating in and ten thousand people write ten letters each, creating 100,000 letters.

And this is the point where the Chain Letter scheme pays off for me. If everything has gone to plan, I will receive £500,000 through the post in £5 notes, as all the recipients send me their money, remove me from the list and add their own names to the bottom of the list. It sounds ridiculous but if everyone plays their part this is a mathematical certainty. Suddenly, I'm rich and all I had to do was post ten letters. That beats working for a living!

In the distant past, Chain Letters made huge sums of money for those at the optimum positions in the lists (more on the positioning later) and the originators of the letter saw the value in ensuring that as many people as possible continued the chain and sent new letters. This lead to the content of some letters taking a disturbing turn, with talk of curses, bad luck and other superstitious nonsense that threatened to ruin the lives of anyone who dared to break the chain. TV campaigns offered to destroy Chain Letters on behalf of viewers that were too scared to do it themselves and the hoax nature of the Chain Letter became so well known that everything fizzled out fairly quickly. The vast majority of people who took part didn't see any money back at all and as you'll see shortly that's a very large number of people.

Whilst the Chain Letter is (now) an illegal scam, it's important to remember that in the example above it all worked out for **me** – I got £500,000 for an afternoon's work. Obviously that means it can work for you, right? Hold that thought. We'll come back to it in a moment.

The Bucket Business.

In order to understand why the Chain Letter is illegal (and rightly so), we need to examine the movement of money and the Bucket Business is a great example of how cash needs a product or service at the heart of any transaction. In this example, I have recently started my own Bucket Business which is a concept I just made up, so I'll explain what that means. I'm heading off out into the streets to drum up business for my bucket. My bucket offers you a fantastic opportunity to make money so if you see me out with my bucket, I'd urge you to come and speak to me, because you've never seen a simpler way to make money easily.

All you have to do is put £1 in my bucket. I will give you a ticket in return and in two weeks time you can come back and exchange your ticket for £50 from the bucket. It really is that simple. You spend £1 and receive £50. You would have to be a fool to pass up this opportunity, right?

The success or failure of the Bucket Business is initially dependent on how many people I can persuade to put a pound in the bucket and most importantly, the exact time and date when the people start to come back to claim their money. The customer must return to me no sooner than two weeks from the time they made their original payment and assuming that 49 other people have taken part in that period, there will be enough money in the bucket for my first ticket holder to take out their £50.

This scheme works for the first few people that take part. After all, the opportunity is incredible – earn back 50 times more than your original stake! And it's only a quid, right? Who wouldn't take part in that? There will be enough money in that bucket to pay me and the first few investors. But let's take look at the overall picture instead of looking at it from the point of view of the individual participants. During the first two weeks of my business venture I persuaded ten thousand people to put money in the bucket. Then, once the two week period had passed, these customers started to come back, each returning their tickets and claiming their £50. I have ten thousand pounds in the bucket so the first two hundred people get their money and they go away happy. Sadly there is no more money in the bucket and the business collapses.

The end result of this ridiculous affair is that I have 9,800 customers who have lost their money, a business that was always worthless and a queue of people outside my door that would like to do me physical harm. However, there are also 200 people who love my Bucket Business and are so convinced that the system works that they cannot wait to recommend me to all their friends and family members. Their belief in the system is so strong that they might even go out and buy a bucket of their own and start a rival business. They have seen with their own eyes that the system works and no-one will be able to convince them that this is a scam.

Those few customers that made a profit don't have any visibility of the thousands of people that lost out, and I can use this to my advantage. If I were to contact each of those customers and offer them another chance to invest, they would surely jump at the chance. Their confidence in the system will make it easy for me to convince them to invest more money. This time, I can suggest each customer invest, say, £5000, and in two weeks time they will be able to claim a quarter of a million pounds in return. Their initial success will provide them with the confidence to make the investment, and I'll not tell them that I'm leaving for Rio de Janeiro in the morning and never coming back.

The Bucket Business is ultimately doomed to fail for one simple reason. There is no product or service to justify the movement of the money. All that is happening is that the money is moving from one location to another. Nothing is actually happening that grows that investment. For one person to make money, another has to lose it.

The movement of money is something we all take for granted and participate in every day. We don't see the complexity because it's all so simple. **The movement of money has to include a product or service to justify the movement**.

If I add a product or service to my Bucket Business it will be more difficult for me to persuade people to give me their cash, because I will struggle to come up with any product that beats "Give me a quid, I'll give you fifty!" as an attractive proposition. I will need to work harder and think about what I can offer to fill a customer need.

Welcome to Bucket Business 2.0. For my new improved business I will stand outside the railway station in the hot summer months and alongside the bucket I will have an ice box filled with cans of refreshing cold drinks for the commuters. When they give me a pound I will give them a drink in return. They will be happy (especially as we know how awful the trains are in the hot summer) and I will have their £1 in my bucket.

When I run out of drinks, I can go to the cash and carry to buy more stock. I'll use the money I take from the commuters to buy more drinks, a bigger ice box and I'll improve my business. The money from the commuters was initially given to them by their employers in exchange for their hard work and then given to me in exchange for drinks. I gave some of it to the cash and carry owner for more stock, he gave some of that money to the drinks company to replenish his stock and some of that money was paid to the employees of the drinks company as payment for their work.

When those employees get thirsty they might choose to buy a drink from my business and the money continues to move around with everyone involved benefitting from their place in the loop. Those that spend the money get the refreshment they crave and those that keep their money may spend it in any other way they choose.

With Chain Letters, my original Bucket Business and other examples of this kind of scam there is no product or service to move money out of the loop into another loop. Without this, all that happens is the money moves around the scam. If one person passes money to the other without the exchange of a product or service then they are out of pocket. The other person made a profit but it had to be at the expense of the first person losing out.

The Mathematics of Big Numbers.

Going back to our Chain Letter, we see how some names on the list made considerable sums of money and at each level of the chain new names were added to the bottom of the list. Each participant stands the chance to continue to make ever increasing amounts of money – right? The sums multiply by ten every time so the maths is very simple.

When I created that chain I put myself at position number five in the list, but based on what we now know, why didn't I put myself further down the list? I earned £500,000 by placing myself at position number five, but if I had put myself at position six I would have five million pounds! To understand the complexities of these logistics, we need to examine something called Exponential Growth, which lies at the heart of Multi Level Marketing, Pyramid Schemes and Chain Letters. The problem with Exponential Growth is that it's been proven that human beings struggle to understand the 'big number' mathematics, even when it's right there in plain sight. Allow me to explain with a game.

THE LITTLE BOOK OF MULTI LEVEL MARKETING

Imagine someone just offered you a job with a highly unusual pay structure. You'd be working in a job you won't enjoy on a one month contract. It's hard work and you'll be miserable for the entire time, so you hope the money will make it worthwhile. At the interview, the boss explains how you will be paid. At the end of the first day you will receive one penny.

One shiny penny.

For all that hard work.

This, as with every other day will be a direct bank transfer so you won't even see it. At the end of the second day your pay will double and you will receive 2p for that day. This happens every day for the one month contract, so after the third day you will be paid 4p, then 8p for the next day and so on.

Before you read on, it's worth noting that on a long enough timeline, this could earn you serious money. Sadly as this job is only a one month contract there is no way to keep working after 31 days, so I'd like you to take a quick guess at how much would be in the bank at the end of the month. Surely this awful job isn't worth taking when you're being paid in pennies?

Keep that guess in your mind and we'll come back to it shortly.

Next, have you ever played Roulette?

Roulette is a very simple gambling game. The player guesses where a ball will land on a rotating wheel. The wheel is surrounded by numbers from 0 – 36, with 18 red numbers, 18 black numbers and a green zero. If the player bets on red or black the house pays back double the stake amount if the ball lands in that colour (for example, a £10 bet pays back £20, which is the original stake plus the same again).

This would be a 50/50 bet if there were no green zero on the wheel and the green number gives the house a slight edge. Without the green zero (and on a long enough timeline) a player would in theory win and lose equally and the game would be pointless. Having the odds slightly in the favour of the casino means that on a long enough timeline you should always lose in the end.

Many years ago, players devised a plan known as "doubling up". To double up, the player starts with an initial bet and if they lose they simply double their stake next time and keep doubling up for every spin of the wheel until they win.

It looks like this:

Place your £10 bet on red.

- If you win, put the £10 winnings in your pocket and start this process again.
- If you lose, stake double the amount of the previous bet and play again.
- Repeat this until you win and when this happens you can put £10 in your pocket and start again.

That seems very simple on paper and in fact the process is so straightforward that it becomes very difficult to see why it would not work. If you follow this process you will always make a profit of £10 whenever a red number spins in. Half of the roulette wheel is made up of red numbers so you're bound to win eventually... although you've already read enough of this book to know there must be a catch.

Let's say you place your first bet and you win. Ten pounds goes into your pocket and you start over. For the next 4 spins of the wheel you lose and so you double the bet each time and on the fifth spin a red number drops and you win. You lost the first four bets (£10, £20, £40, £80) and you're seriously out of pocket. But the fifth bet won and as you bet £160, you collected £320. Your total outlay including the previous losses was £310, you just won £320 and so you're £10 up. You put that £10 in the pocket and start the process again.

Doubling up on roulette is fascinating because when you first learn of the process it seems too good to be true. It is simple maths and this makes it very difficult to see how it wouldn't work. Every time a red number comes up you win back everything you spent, plus an extra £10 that goes in your pocket. How can it go wrong?

THE LITTLE BOOK OF MULTI LEVEL MARKETING

It's all down to the Exponential Growth that I mentioned earlier. The problem with this kind of growth is that the numbers get bigger quickly and can easily become out of control.

Remember the job puzzle earlier? You'd earn 1p for a day's work, then 2p, then 4p and so on? How much did you guess you could earn in a month? Most people think that after 31 days they would have accumulated £5 or £10 in copper coins, but the reality often comes as a shock. On day 31 alone you would receive a pay packet of over ten million pounds (£10,737,418 and 24 pence to be precise). And this would be for that single day; you'd have earned nearly the same amount already over the previous month.

The pay packet started in pennies, but as the number doubles each day it doesn't take long for the numbers to increase drastically. Day one may only earn you a penny, but day 10 earns you £5.12, which is still terrible money for a day's work but is 512 times more than you earned only 9 days earlier. By day 20, you're earning £5,542 for the day, £10,485 for day 21, £20,971 for day 22 and so on. You earn over 1.3 million pounds on day 28 alone and 2.6 million on day 29, 5.3 million on day 30 and the aforementioned 10.7 million on the last day. Ten million pounds for one day's work! Sign me up, I'm available!

Back to the roulette wheel and the small numbers get out of control here as well. On a long enough timeline a roulette wheel will spin a black or red result a similar number of times and we assume that the results will be a constant mixture of red and black numbers. Statistically, a streak of 10 black numbers in a row is no more or less likely than any other sequence of results. If the mixture of results shows a roughly even number of wins and losses, the doubling up process will work to some extent.

As soon as you have a few losses in a row the whole scheme starts to fall apart. You find yourself betting £80, £160, £320, £640, £1280, all in the hope that at some point a red number will fall into place. It's true that if this happens, you'll be a winner, but it only takes 8 losses in a row for you to be betting £2560 in the hope of winning an extra £10 overall. You'd never wager like this normally, but in doubling up you may be forced to.

While we are here and we're wagering these high stakes, we should check the house rules to see if they have an upper limit for the table. Players experimenting with doubling up may experience a moment of panic when the house doesn't accept their next bet. The game comes to an abrupt halt. The house always wins.

Ok, I get it, but what's this got to do with Multi Level Marketing?

You're right, it's taken a little time to get here – but it was all important. These examples show how the human brain can be tricked, or at least manipulated into missing important information. With Exponential Growth, our brains are not prepared for the incredible rate that these numbers will increase. At the same time the logic behind Chain Letters and doubling up appears sound. It's very difficult to take a step back and examine the scheme from an overall point of view, especially when you are right in the middle of the action.

Sensible, intelligent people may read the double up process over and over again and only realise that it doesn't work when it's too late and they've lost money. These same sensible, intelligent people would turn down the job that pays 1p for the first day because human beings are not wired to fully understand the power of Exponential Growth. People may be tempted to send £5 to a random name on a Chain Letter in the hope of receiving millions of fivers back in return. Getting involved in these schemes doesn't mean you are a fool – the method seems sound on paper and by the time you can see the flaws it's often too late.

Before we get on specifically to the Multi Level Marketing, let's quickly return back to the Chain Letter example. By strategically placing my own name at position number five I made a good return, but as alluded to earlier I could have positioned my name at number six and gained ten times that amount of money back. Or I could have put my name at position number ten and earned billions of pounds! So why did I choose to put myself so comparatively low in the order?

The answer is that the Chain Letter is going to grow exponentially in the same way as all the other examples we have looked at. **I need everyone involved to send me their money before the whole scheme collapses.** The Chain Letter is doomed to fail right from the start, just as my Bucket Business had to. There are no products or services in the Chain Letter so the money is simply moving from one person to another. As with the Bucket Business, the people at the top of the list make a profit and the people below them must be losing out.

Starting at the fifth position in the list, my name rose to the top at the point when there were 100,000 letters in circulation, netting me £500,000. The next level involves a million letters being sent. In the UK, that's a letter being posted to one in every 63 people (including children). If we continue this, those people would be writing to 10 million people, who in turn would need to write to 100 million, then a billion, then 10 billion people. We've exceeded the population of the whole world now. The numbers have got out of control and if you're the individual that's adding their name to the list and sending £5 then I'm very sorry but there's **absolutely no way your name will ever get to the top of the list**. Even if you were the first person in the chain to receive my letter, adding your name in position number ten leaves you too low in the pyramid to have any chance of receiving money. Your £5 may as well be going into my bucket, because you will never see it again. The system simply does not work, but the

theory makes sense and this is why intelligent people fall for the scam.

In today's world we are more connected than ever. We share updates about our lives on Facebook, Twitter, Instagram, Snapchat, Myspace and Bebo (OK, maybe not those last two) and we have the opportunity to be in contact with people in more ways than ever before. We no longer write letters like we used to and the Chain Letter scam has all but disappeared. However, in the early days of the internet there was a resurgence of people trying to start their own Chain Letter scams via email and in the modern day, Multi Level Marketing has become increasingly visible on social media. Could Multi Level Marketing be the latest money making scam? Let's find out.

What is Multi Level Marketing?

Multi Level Marketing differs from traditional retailing by offering the opportunity for salespeople to recruit other salespeople to work under them. Initially, you may be approached by a friend or relative who has become involved in a scheme where they sell products. You might choose to buy this product from your friend and become a customer. This is traditional retailing - your friend buys a product wholesale, then sells that product to you individually and makes a profit. ==The difference with Multi Level Marketing (MLM) is that your friend can also offer you the opportunity to become a distributor for that product yourself.== If you choose to do so, you can sell the product to your friends and family, but you can also recruit people to sell the product, in just the same way as your friend recruited you. Each distributor at every level is encouraged to recruit a team that works under them and earns money from each sale their team makes.

What is the difference between MLM and a pyramid scheme?

I'm glad you asked. The Chain Letter and Bucket Business are both pyramids in their own way. In a pyramid scheme there is no product or service. The investment you make goes into the scheme itself. This means that the entire business runs on money simply moving from one person to another. Therefore if anyone profits from the scheme, someone else has to lose out. Pyramid schemes are illegal in the UK and for good reason. As with the Bucket Business and Chain Letters, those at the top of the pyramid stand to make an incredible amount of money, but this has to come at the expense of those lower down the chain.

Pyramid schemes get their name from the organisational layout of the company. An individual creates the scheme and recruits people to work for them. Each of those people will recruit other people to work under them, resulting in a larger number of people in the next level of the business. At each level, the people continue to recruit other people to work under them, making the pyramid shape wider still.

With all of this in mind, you can see that there are many similarities between MLM schemes and pyramid schemes. The two major differences are that (a) pyramid schemes are illegal in the UK and (b) **MLMs are based around selling of products**, as well as further recruitment.

With so many similarities between the structure of a pyramid scheme and that of an MLM, it's worth exploring what proportion of the salesperson's profit is achieved by sales of the product only. If a salesperson makes, say, 90% of their money selling a product and 10% by recruiting other people to join then that sounds like a good, growing business. But if each salesperson finds they make all of their money through recruitment and barely make any money selling the product then how does that differ from a pyramid scheme? This is where the structure of an MLM becomes really intriguing because if the whole business is based on recruitment then there's no need for the product other than to provide legal legitimacy to the endeavour.

The big question becomes, **if a Multi Level Marketing Company uses the pyramid model to sell products and recruit people, but no-one actually ever buys the product, does it stop being an MLM and become an illegal pyramid scheme?**

To understand MLM marketing, you need to take a step back from what you see at your own position in the company and look at the overall business. It can be incredibly difficult to see the world from an overall view instead of a personal one but it's vital to do so if you want to understand the risks of becoming involved in MLM.

As a thought exercise and to demonstrate how tricky it can be to take that step back, consider this story. A disease has broken out which kills anyone who has it. There are no symptoms to this illness but if you have it, you'll suddenly drop dead at some point in the next six months. There's no cure, but you'll need to know if you have this disease or not – the last thing you need is to drop dead in the street. The disease only affects one in every 100,000 people, but as there are no symptoms the only way to find out if you have it is to visit the

Doctor. He reassures you that you're probably fine, but there is a test you can take to be sure. The test is 99% accurate, the results come back in 24 hours and it will be a weight off your mind to know you're OK. You take the test and pop back to the Doctor the next day. He isn't smiling. Sadly your test came back positive. It says you have the disease and you'll be dead in six months.

Based on the paragraph above, most people would go and hug their loved ones and start putting their affairs in order. But really, how likely is it that you have the disease? Read it again if you need to before continuing. It's a great example of how we struggle to see the world from a different point of view.

The two key points here are that the test is only 99% accurate and the disease statistically only affects one in every 100,000 people. From our individual point of view we see a 99% effective test as being as close to 100% accurate as can be. But this is a national pandemic! The story is not about us individually, it's about a disease. Every time a patient takes the test there is a 1% chance that the result is not accurate. Therefore, if

> 100,000 people go to the doctor, statistically we know that only one will have the disease, yet 1000 people will get an inaccurate reading.

You have a 1 in 1000 chance of having the disease. The '99% accurate' statistic is useless unless you know it was 100% accurate on the occasion when you took the test.

Human beings live in the centre of their own universe. It makes it very difficult to understand our situation from a different point of view. We struggle to see where we fit in the overall MLM business structure when we are introduced to a money making opportunity by a smiling, trusted friend. We don't worry about the complexities of big number mathematics, Exponential Growth, the movement of money and all the underlying issues that can cause our MLM experience to be an unpleasant one.

"**So lovely to see you! It's been ages. Tell me all your news.**"

MLMs are usually introduced into the conversation by friends or family members, so it can be difficult to keep an overall view of the situation when it all seems so... personal. One of the reasons that you allow someone to be your friend is that you trust them and MLMs can really benefit from this. If a random person on the street offers you a great money making opportunity you might well run a mile, but if you're having a beer with a friend, putting the world to rights and the conversation happens to turn to money, it feels like a normal chat with a friend. It doesn't come across as the sales pitch that it really is.

I was presented with a MLM conversation at a 'family fun day' where I was working as a magician. It started as an informal chat with a lady who was a stallholder at the event. On the day, I was performing magic and selling the tricks, which is hard work and repetitive. It's important for me to keep my energy and enthusiasm up as I perform the same magic trick for the 50th time. I was showing off a magic colouring book (a book that colours in by itself and has pages that turn blank on command) and this lady came over. She asked me where I got my energy from and commented that she could see from her stall that I was working hard, generating a crowd and making money. I explained I used to work for a large corporation in an office environment and here I was messing about with magic tricks – to me, this wasn't hard work.

"Still", she said, "It's amazing for me to see this. Your energy and enthusiasm hasn't let up since we started."

She was right and I do get focussed in my work. I try to give the customer my entire attention and sometimes I get lost in my own bubble. I rarely look at other people's stalls and I definitely hadn't seen her stall because if I had, I'd have seen what was coming next.

The lady continued to watch me, bought some of my stock and made very complimentary comments about what she had seen. At the end of the day she came back over. I wondered if I'd pulled. Sadly it was not to be and she instead continued with the compliments. She told me she'd been speaking to her boss about me. My infectious enthusiasm was just what their company was looking for. She asked me more about my old office job and offered loaded questions, "So you'd work long hours, yeah? I bet it was stressful". Ultimately, she explained that there was a vacancy for me with her company and if I wanted to apply I'd walk it. She set up a webcast meeting with her boss, sent me an invitation by email and the following week I sat with my laptop, coffee at the ready, eager to find out all about this opportunity.

The presentation started with an explanation of the product. The lady worked for a utility company and had bundled her gas, electricity, telephone and broadband into one convenient monthly bill. It saved her money over her old suppliers and she loved the product so much that she had started recommending it to other people. She had gone on to sign up as an independent distributor with a 'downline'. As soon as I heard the word 'downline', I realised that her flattery had indeed got her somewhere, because I was sat in my house on a MLM recruitment conference cast and I couldn't believe I'd fallen for it.

The 'downline' is a piece of MLM speak that forms the basis of the potential earnings. Picturing the pyramid shape we discussed earlier, each person in the pyramid has people above them and below them. If I signed up for this utility company, the woman that introduced me would be the first person in my 'upline,' and if I recruited anyone to join the scheme, these people would be in my team and would form my 'downline'. As with many MLMs, if any of those people also recruited other people then they would be in my 'downline' as well.

By signing up for the utility company I would enter into a 12 month contract for all my services and I would pay a monthly fee. The lady that signed me up would receive a small amount of money each month for as long as I remained a customer of the utility company. Therefore it stood to reason that if I recruited anyone, she would also get a small cut of that each month as well. The structure of the business mirrored aspects of the Chain Letter, with each level of the chain making money for those in the upline. If I joined, the people above me would make money and if I recruited people I would make money from those below me. If I could recruit 5 people and they recruited 5 people (and they in turn recruited 5 people) my profits could grow... exponentially! Suddenly, it's all starting to sound quite familiar.

An MLM scheme based around household bills is a good universal product choice. However, in research for this book I have attended similar presentations for fashion brands, cosmetics, skincare products, book distribution, household cleaning products – you name it, there's an MLM for it - and the presentations can feel remarkably similar to each other regardless of the product.

As explained earlier, with MLMs you have to take a step back and stop looking at the situation from your personal point of view in order to see the entire structure. When the lady came over to talk to me at the market stall it felt like a personal conversation between two people. The reality of the situation is that this lady was at the event with her own utility company stall. She'd figured that this event would be a good way to meet and recruit people and was using flattery and a friendly attitude to get them to sign up for the conference webcast. When these people saw the presentation, she hoped that they would join the scheme and she'd make money. If they went on to recruit other people, she'd make even more money.

The conversation we'd had made me feel special. The bigger picture was that she was recruiting anyone and everyone she spoke to all day and many of these people ended up on that webcast. She'd done a good job!

The web conference rang alarm bells and I came away from the presentation convinced this was a pyramid scheme. The presenter spent only a few minutes discussing the benefits of switching to the utility company and the majority of the time was spent talking about the recruitment opportunities. The lady I'd spoken to was featured in the slide presentation, showing how she had quit her job as a teacher to promote the utility company full time. It explained her potential 'on-target earnings', a completely meaningless figure that shows what you could earn if you achieve your 'target'. But who sets the target and is it achievable? Imagine being, say, a hunter, with the potential to earn ten million pounds in 'on target earnings', but your target is to capture a Bigfoot, a Dodo and the Loch Ness Monster. It's a huge tempting sum of money, but you have no chance at all of getting your hands on it.

The real crusher for me was that I'd wasted an hour of my time watching this presentation and really felt like I'd been suckered in by the charm and flattery. Since then, I've seen this utility company all over the place and I've had similar flattering conversations, always a different person doing the spiel and always filled with highly complementary comments about my own business and enthusiasm. And because we've already discussed exponential growth it makes sense that there are so many people out there trying to recruit me. We've already seen how these numbers can get out of control quickly, but with so many people promoting the company, is there anyone in this area that hasn't had the same conversation with one of these people?

Why do people fall for it?

I'm fascinated by one particular fact about MLMs. If the focus of the business is for salespeople to recruit and the salesperson earns money from recruiting other people (who in turn earn more money by recruiting more people) is there anyone that will give you an honest answer when you ask them if it's worthwhile?

Looking at the evidence from the conference webcast I attended, the idea of the business is for everyone involved to recruit five people each. If they do, they will make money from those people. Surely this is the reason why everyone you speak to is so positive? The ex-teacher had given up a well paid job and was set to earn a huge amount of money if she hit her targets, but were those targets achievable? If I looked her straight in the eye and asked the question, "Seriously – are you really making any money at all from this venture?" would she even contemplate for a second saying no? Of course not! She's trying to recruit me to make the same decisions that she made when she joined. She could be like a bad gambler, chasing her losses, desperately trying to claw some of her expenses back by recruiting more people.

The whole experience of talking to this person felt like a normal conversation but afterwards I could tell that her life revolved around trying to recruit almost everyone she met. I imagine that when she goes on holiday she takes photographs specifically to post online to show what a great holiday she is having, because... you know... you can do this too! You can live the same incredible lifestyle as this lady who spends her weekends hanging around near the bouncy castle at a 'family fun day', desperately trying to recruit people to switch their energy provider. Project an image of success, show everyone your fantastic lifestyle in the hope that others will aspire to achieve your level of greatness and perhaps they will sign up and you'll make some money from this awful venture, finally!

The world of MLMs is awash with video clips of successful entrepreneurs flashing the cash, driving the expensive sports cars and sipping champagne on beautiful beaches. It's incredibly alluring and it's easy for people to be drawn in. The friend, family member or stranger that introduces you to this world needs to present an image of their own success, otherwise why would anyone else buy into the scheme? On that basis, how can you possibly expect to get an honest answer from anyone involved in the system when their pay packet is directly linked to getting you involved?

The language of the MLM matches the situation of the individual being recruited. When I said I'd quit an office job, I was told how great the MLM opportunity would be because I could choose my own hours, be independent, work without stress and so on. Everything I criticised about office life was turned around and presented back at me as a benefit of MLM. If I said I wanted to spend more time hammering six inch nails into my scalp, I'm sure the lady would have told me how MLM could help me achieve this.

I believe it is for this reason that I see so many people from different walks of life getting involved in MLMs. I find it incredibly prevalent when I pick up the kids from primary school. Being surrounded by young parents who have recently gone back into work after maternity, the MLM lifestyle has really struck a chord with a large number of these young mums. The flexible hours, home working opportunities and social networking that comes with the package make it sound like an ideal match.

Of course, young mums also tend to know a lot of other young mums and so they feel it will be easy for them to recruit enough people to make it worth their while. I estimate about half the people I talk to at the school gates are involved in some sort of MLM and everyone speaks about how great it is and how I should do it too. Despite this, I see no evidence around me of this success and I wonder how, if Jean really is making so much money from her MLM, why she's still driving that old car?

MLMs are often beautifully presented, using language and imagery that is designed to appeal to specific demographics. If you're a new mum, this is perfect for you! If you're a stressed out office worker, this is perfect for you. Whatever your situation, this is perfect for you! I'm confident that if you tell them you're a Cyberdyne Systems T-1000 from the future on a mission to kill John Connor, they'll tell you that this opportunity is perfect for you too! This is a business that you can fit around your day - Hunt and kill Sarah Connor (so that her son John will never be born) in the morning, pick the kids up from school at 3pm and spend a couple of hours in between working from home in this exciting new venture! You'll be perfect for this role, with your charisma, your charm, your circle of friends, your shoes, your clothes and your motorcycle.

The evidence - Why MLMs must surely fail.

We've looked at the mathematics of big numbers and how Chain Letters and Exponential Growth can go completely out of control very quickly. Using the maths of the utility company I mentioned earlier, here's why I believe that the business cannot possibly be sustained and why I believe the lady I spoke to was lying about how much money she was making.

The first step into the MLM process would have been to switch my gas, electric, telephone and broadband to the new company. This would potentially save me some money, but that tends to be true for most companies whether MLM or not. Switching your energy and landline provider to save money is always a good idea if you are out of contract, so this alone didn't interest me (I happened to be on a good deal I'd received from my previous supplier and so switching would not have saved me any money anyway). However, it seemed that this was not a problem and I could still earn money by recruiting even if I was not a customer myself. This screamed out "pyramid scheme!" to me, but if I had signed up, my next goal would be to sign up five more people.

This is where we need to take a step back and look at the overall picture. I'm being asked to find 5 people, but how many other recruiters are doing the same? What are the chances of me finding 5 people who haven't already had this conversation?

Someone, at some point in the past, founded this company as an MLM and recruited some salespeople. Let's say they recruited 5 people to keep our math straightforward. At the top of the pyramid shape there is the company founder and below them there are the 5 people he recruited. These people are level 2 of the pyramid shape. Each of these 5 people recruits 5 more people. From their individual point of view they now have 5 people in their downline, but this is misleading because there are 20 other people at this 3rd level of the pyramid shape.

The people at level three recruit 5 people each, which will create 125 new recruits at level 4 of the pyramid. If this continues there will be 625 new recruits at level 5, another 3,125 at level 6, an extra 15,625 at level 7 and another 78,125 at level 8.

It gets worse. Level 9 introduces another 390,625 people to the scheme, who in turn will need to recruit 1,953,125 people to keep it going.

Level 11 requires the recruiters to find another 9.7 million people, level 12 involves recruiting almost every remaining man woman and child in the UK (an extra 48,828,125 people to be precise) and level 13 has us desperately searching to recruit anyone in the world (another 244 million people).

If this business is to keep growing, we need over a billion new people to join (1,220,703,125) at level 14 and at level 15 we need to recruit an additional six billion, one hundred and three million, five hundred and fifteen thousand, six hundred and twenty five people to keep this going. You've asked all your family, all your friends, but there's no-one left in the world, every single person on the planet is trying to recruit every other person. It's not adding up! And let's be honest here. There are some people who won't want to join your MLM, no matter how great your sales technique. The Queen, for example is far too busy. So is Prince Charles. Simon Cowell has enough money already – he doesn't need this.

We saw earlier how doubling up can make numbers go out of control quickly and in recruiting 5 people you're effectively quintupling up. Is it any wonder that so many people at the school gates are trying to promote these MLMs to me, how every event I perform magic at has a stand for this company, that company.... everyone's at it!

So how do you make the money?

The simple answer is you are more likely to lose money than make money. Someone has to pay for the cars, the holidays and the fabulous lifestyles of those at the top of the pyramid so for them to make money it must come from somewhere – and that is from you! If you do join one of these schemes, how far down the pyramid shape are you before you even begin? How can you find out? I could ask the lady at the utility company, but how is she supposed to know where she fits? Could she go back to the person who recruited her and find out who recruited them and play detective all the way back up the pyramid?

Stepping back and seeing the whole picture you can tell that if you are in the business at the **very** start you can make serious money and the more people below you, the more money you can make. This would explain the enticing recruitment videos of people steering jet skis over clear blue waters next to sandy beaches. With each level of the pyramid shape there are exponentially more people involved in the scheme and that means there is less money to be made at each level. By the time it reaches you, you are surely too far down to make any level of money that makes your efforts worthwhile. As with the Bucket Business and the Chain Letter there is an optimum position to be and I'm sorry to say that those positions were probably filled a long time ago.

The only solution seems to be that you should start your own MLM business, rather than joining an existing one. But knowing what you know about the numbers, would you honestly feel comfortable in setting up your own company, knowing that other people will have to suffer for you to get rich?

And what happens to the product?

With recruitment numbers growing exponentially it can feel like everyone in the world is selling an MLM product. But if everyone's selling, who's buying? This is a key issue that needs addressing.

Some MLM businesses allow the salesperson to work their way up through a series of levels within the business, increasing their status in the company as they go. This can involve achieving specific sales targets for the product and a distributor that purchases a certain amount of product each month can achieve the honour of being, say, a Bronze team member. As their business expands they can work their way up to the Silver level and achieve benefits from doing so. This continues through the Gold level, Platinum level, Double Platinum, Double Gold Happy Platinum, Great Big Happy Triple Platinum Excitement Plus and many other spurious names of levels that I just made up. The problem is that each distributor can be tempted to spend money on stock purely to maintain their level in the company, knowing that they don't have enough customers to sell it to.

But who are their customers anyway? If the distributor is doing an effective job then their customers will want to become distributors themselves. That should be exactly what the distributor is hoping will happen but this outcome represents one less customer to buy the stock. Therefore, if the number of distributors grows exponentially, the potential number of customers must be shrinking exponentially as well. With that in mind, who's buying and using the product?

Many MLM distributors are passionate about the product and choose to 'be the brand' and live the lifestyle values of the company. If their MLM is a range of skincare products they might proudly tell everyone how they use the products themselves every day. Many MLM products are genuinely good quality and the sales message from a beautiful woman with great skin means a lot when they tell you they are using the product every day. It creates the image that the distributor isn't just selling the product but endorsing it – they become an ambassador for the brand.

Viewed from another angle, the distributor might well be using the product because they have a large quantity of stock on hand and they are struggling to sell it. Everyone's a salesperson in this business so no-one's left to buy! The system starts to fall down when the distributor realises that they are buying stock in quantities that allow them to maintain their executive level, without necessarily having customers to sell the product to.

Initial sales when joining an MLM can also be misleading. When a distributor is advised to target friends and family to join the scheme they will make initial sales because friends and family do nice things for each other. Your mum may express an interest in the products you are selling but is that a genuine enthusiasm for the product or are they just trying to help their loved one be successful? Those initial good sales may not be sustainable as your MLM stops being a new venture and becomes business-as-usual. Your friends may well place orders with you at first but if they are only doing this to help out there will probably not be the level of repeat business you expect.

Again, running a business in this way is clearly unsustainable. Buying stock is only worthwhile if you can sell that stock and if the main focus of your business is recruiting other people to do the same thing, the stock can end up stored in the garage in the hope that it will sell at some point in the future. For products with a use-by date, their finite life span means that it becomes worthless after a specific timeframe. Product ends up being thrown away because the product was never the focus of the MLM in the first place. The product was merely a structure to hang the pyramid scheme onto.

And the saddest part of all. People may not want to be your friend any more.

This is the worst aspect of the MLM system. When someone introduces you to the business, they are very positive about the rewards you can achieve, the generous pay packet and the many benefits of being your own boss, working your own hours and so on. However, we have established that they will benefit financially if you sign up to the scheme so they are unlikely to say *"Honestly? It's a waste of time, I'm working my backside off and making no money at all"*, if they are trying to recruit you!

But this person is your friend. If you do sign up, you'll be trying to recruit your friends and family and if they sign up they will be one layer lower down in the pyramid than you. If you're not making any money, they are making even less than that! Before you know it, you'll realise that your friend may not have been entirely honest with you about their earnings and once you understand that, you may resent them for getting you involved in the scheme in the first place. The problem is, by the time you're in that position, you will have probably signed up other members of your social circle and they are likely to be having the same feelings about you. MLMs can cause rifts across families and communities and it's very sad.

The Sunk Cost Fallacy

We've looked at the ways that MLMs can seem plausible on paper and how the human brain finds it difficult to follow the exponential growth of numbers. I'd like to touch upon one other way that your brain works against you – the Sunk Cost Fallacy. You may have experienced this in other areas of life because the SCF is everywhere. If you've ever played one of those building games on your phone or tablet that hooks you in, you'll be familiar with it. If you've ever thrown good money after bad, you'll know. The SCF is a trick that your mind plays on you when you know you should give up but you have already invested too much time, money, effort or all three.

I'm all too familiar with the SCF. I've been playing a game on my phone for a while now and it's a masterpiece of psychological manipulation. The object of the game is to build a lemonade stall and every time you tap the screen on the tablet you sell some lemonade. When you have earned enough money, you can open another stall and another, until you have enough money to build a different kind of stall. There are 10 different types of stall and when you have enough money you can automate each stall and that's when you start to see the money increasing really quickly.

After a few weeks of playing you have everything automated and at this point you realise you can reset the whole game and you will start again but with a 4X score multiplier. I did this and the next time I played the money shot up. I was able to rebuild back to where I was previously within a couple of days and my in-game bank balance was in the millions of pounds. Eventually the game gave me the opportunity to restart again, this time with an 8x bonus. My score ended in the quintillions, the sexdecillions, the septendillions and when I got the chance to restart again, this time with a 'who-knows-how-blooming-high' multiplier, I went for it.

My score was reaching the sexseptendillions when I had a huge wave of clarity washing over me. This game was no fun at all. I'd done everything the game had to offer, weeks ago. All that was happening was my score was getting ludicrously big and this was surely never going to reach an end point. What a complete waste of all that time! The thing is, even with that realisation, I've carried on playing. I've spent money on in-game purchases to make the score go up even quicker and I can't bring myself to leave it alone. The reason is the SCF. My brain is telling me, "yes, this is a load of rubbish, but you can't stop now! Think of all the time and money you spent to get here!"

The SCF is especially prevalent in the world of MLMs, where you are surrounded by people who are doing well in the business (or at least that is what they are telling you). You feel like the whole thing isn't working, you've spent and lost money, you're struggling to get people to sign up to your scheme and you really should just quit. But something in the back of your mind won't let go. You can't be the only one not making money? Your friend has been doing this longer than you and they always say what a great scheme it is! If you quit now, all that hard work was for nothing!

People in MLMs may advise you to push through the hard times and to keep going. Of course, anyone with a vested interest in your recruitment will say this. If you quit, they won't make any money from you so it's in the interests of everyone around you to keep you in the game. This is a problem. You want to quit, you need to quit and no-one will let you. One MLM meeting I attended devoted a whole section to ways of dealing with negative people.

"There will be people who say to you, give it up, it's a worthless pyramid scheme! Well, how do you think they will feel when they see you on your own private yacht? Green with envy? Don't listen to the naysayers! You're on the way up and it feels good!"

Schemes like these do not want you to leave, they want you to stay – you're earning money for everyone in your upline. If it's not working out for you (and we've seen the reasons why it probably isn't) then perhaps it's time to give it up before it costs you even more time and money? You'll be glad to be rid of it, even though it will feel difficult to give up. All that work, all that time, all that effort, all that money, all for nothing. It will hurt, but imagine doing this for another year, still making no money and then giving up. You'll be wishing you'd quit a year ago.

In Summary

In writing this short book, I've tried to present an honest opinion of why I feel many Multi Level Marketing schemes are a waste of your time and effort (and not least, your money). Over the past couple of years I have been concerned with the epic rise in numbers, both in the volume of people taking part in these schemes and in the number of businesses offering MLM as a distribution system. Since then, I've started working at events, markets and family fun days and I'm genuinely alarmed at how many of the same businesses I see at these events.

It seems everyone wants me to change my energy provider, use a skin care range, buy children's books or get fit with nutritional shakes. Yet in all of these situations I keep seeing the same process. They talk to the customer about the product then segue into a discussion about life, work, kids, stress, money and end up recommending the business of selling the product, rather than the product itself.

I'm curious to know how much (if any) of the actual product gets sold because these businesses seem all about the recruitment, with the product itself taking a back seat. We've seen in this book how 'recruiting to recruit' is unsustainable and how the number of people required to do that gets out of control very quickly, but I've also seen first-hand the damage to family relationships that can be caused by MLM schemes, as people recommend products and lifestyles to their friends and families, lose money, then lose those friends for the same reason. It can seem incredible that a worldwide, successful MLM company can operate completely legally even though their business model shares so many similarities with the pyramid scheme model.

However, this book has been written with one simple idea behind it. This is a quick read, 11,000 words of how pyramid schemes are surely doomed to failure. I wanted to write a book that could be read quickly in one session that would outline the basic reasons why the schemes look appealing and explain why I feel you're better off leaving them well alone. I hope that this short read helped. If you know someone who is getting involved in a pyramid scheme, please pass this book on. It's available for free to download from Amazon Kindle Unlimited and in paperback for however cheaply I can get it printed.

If this book helps you, please leave a review on Amazon. Pass your copy on to someone else. If they pass it on to their friends and family (who in turn pass it on to their friends and family!) then this information could help them as well. And they can pass it on too. We can use the pyramid model for good! And within just a few levels, this book could have been read by everyone on earth and no-one will ever lose money, or friends, by joining a rotten MLM scheme, ever again.

Thanks for reading.

Printed in Great Britain
by Amazon